LIFE
Lessons

WITH MAX LUCADO

BOOK OF PHILIPPIANS

GUIDE TO JOY

MAX LUCADO

D0108169

Prepared by

THE LIVINGSTONE CORPORATION

Published by

THOMAS NELSON™

Since 1798

www.thomasnelson.com

LIFE *Lessons*

WITH MAX LUCADO

CONTENTS

HOW TO STUDY THE BIBLE

This is a peculiar book you are holding. Words crafted in another language. Deeds done in a distant era. Events recorded in a far-off land. Counsel offered to a foreign people. This is a peculiar book.

It's surprising that anyone reads it. It's too old. Some of its writings date back five thousand years. It's too bizarre. The book speaks of incredible floods, fires, earthquakes, and people with supernatural abilities. It's too radical. The Bible calls for undying devotion to a carpenter who called himself God's Son.

Logic says this book shouldn't survive. Too old, too bizarre, too radical.

The Bible has been banned, burned, scoffed, and ridiculed. Scholars have mocked it as foolish. Kings have branded it as illegal. A thousand times over, the grave has been dug and the dirge has begun, but somehow the Bible never stays in the grave. Not only has it survived; it has thrived. It is the single most popular book in all of history. It has been the best-selling book in the world for years!

There is no way on earth to explain it. Which perhaps is the only explanation. The answer? The Bible's durability is not found on earth; it is found in heaven. For the millions who have tested its claims and claimed its promises, there is but one answer: the Bible is God's book and God's voice.

As you read it, you would be wise to give some thought to two questions. What is the purpose of the Bible? and How do I study the Bible? Time spent reflecting on these two issues will greatly enhance your Bible study.

What is the purpose of the Bible?

Let the Bible itself answer that question.

Since you were a child you have known the Holy Scriptures which are able to make you wise. And that wisdom leads to salvation through faith in Christ Jesus. (2 Tim. 3:15 NCV)

The purpose of the Bible? Salvation. God's highest passion is to get his children home. His book, the Bible, describes his plan of salvation. The purpose of the Bible is to proclaim God's plan and passion to save his children.

That is the reason this book has endured through the centuries. It dares to tackle the toughest questions about life: Where do I go after I die? Is there a God? What do I do with my fears? The Bible offers answers to these crucial questions. It is the treasure map that leads us to God's highest treasure, eternal life.

But how do we use the Bible? Countless copies of Scripture sit unread on bookshelves and nightstands simply because people don't know how to read it. What can we do to make the Bible real in our lives?

QG 11-17-16

The clearest answer is found in the words of Jesus. He promised:

Ask, and God will give to you. Search, and you will find. Knock, and the door will open for you. (Matt. 7:7 NCV)

The first step in understanding the Bible is asking God to help us. We should read prayerfully. If anyone understands God's Word, it is because of God and not the reader.

But the Helper will teach you everything and will cause you to remember all that I told you. The Helper is the Holy Spirit whom the Father will send in my name. (John 14:26 NCV)

Before reading the Bible, pray. Invite God to speak to you. Don't go to Scripture looking for your idea; go searching for his.

Not only should we read the Bible prayerfully; we should read it carefully. *Search and you will find* is the pledge. The Bible is not a newspaper to be skimmed but rather a mine to be quarried.

Search for it like silver, and hunt for it like hidden treasure. Then you will understand respect for the LORD, and you will find that you know God. (Prov. 2:4–5 NCV)

Any worthy find requires effort. The Bible is no exception. To understand the Bible you don't have to be brilliant, but you must be willing to roll up your sleeves and search.

Be a worker who is not ashamed and who uses the true teaching in the right way. (2 Tim. 2:15 NCV)

Here's a practical point. Study the Bible a bit at a time. Hunger is not satisfied by eating twenty-one meals in one sitting once a week. The body needs a steady diet to remain strong. So does the soul. When God sent food to his people in the wilderness, he didn't provide loaves already made. Instead, he sent them manna in the shape of *"thin flakes like frost . . . on the desert ground"* (Ex. 16:14 NCV).

God gave manna in limited portions. God sends spiritual food the same way. He opens the heavens with just enough nutrients for today's hunger. He provides *"a command here, a command there. A rule here, a rule there. A little lesson here, a little lesson there"* (Isa. 28:10 NCV).

Don't be discouraged if your reading reaps a small harvest. Some days a lesser portion is all that is needed. What is important is to search every day for that day's message. A steady diet of God's Word over a lifetime builds a healthy soul and mind.

A little girl returned from her first day at school. Her mom asked, "Did you learn anything?"

"Apparently not enough," the girl responded, "I have to go back tomorrow and the next day and the next . . ."

Such is the case with learning. And such is the case with Bible study. Understanding comes little by little over a lifetime.

There is a third step in understanding the Bible. After the asking and seeking comes the knocking. After you ask and search, then knock.

Knock, and the door will open for you. (Matt. 7:7 NCV)

To knock is to stand at God's door. To make yourself available. To climb the steps, cross the porch, stand at the doorway, and volunteer. Knocking goes beyond the realm of thinking and into the realm of acting.

To knock is to ask, What can I do? How can I obey? Where can I go?

It's one thing to know what to do. It's another to do it. But for those who do it, those who choose to obey, a special reward awaits them.

The truly happy are those who carefully study God's perfect law that makes people free, and they continue to study it. They do not forget what they heard, but they obey what God's teaching says. Those who do this will be made happy. (James 1:25 NCV)

What a promise. Happiness comes to those who do what they read! It's the same with medicine. If you only read the label but ignore the pills, it won't help. It's the same with food. If you only read the recipe but never cook, you won't be fed. And it's the same with the Bible. If you only read the words but never obey, you'll never know the joy God has promised.

Ask. Search. Knock. Simple, isn't it? Why don't you give it a try? If you do, you'll see why you are holding the most remarkable book in history.

INTRODUCTION TO THE BOOK OF PHILIPPIANS

In an era marked by frustration, could you use more contentment? In a world booby-trapped with trouble, could you stand a little more joy?

Come with me back in history a couple of thousand years. We're headed for the city of Rome, that thrilling metropolis of gladiators, chariots, and empires. But we won't stop at the coliseum or palace. We'll travel rather to a drab little room, surrounded by high walls. We'll imagine that we can peek into the room. There we'll see a man seated on the floor. He's an older fellow, balding with shoulders stooped. Chains encircle his hands and feet. And chained to him is a burly Roman guard.

This is the apostle Paul. The tireless church planter who has traveled all over the world. The preacher who has liberated people in every port. The servant of God bound only by the will of God is now in chains—stuck in a dingy house—attached to a Roman officer.

Surely this is a fellow who has every reason to be in a slump!

He is restricted by walls. He is afflicted by friends (1:15). He is conflicted by danger (1:21).

Look closely. He appears to be writing a letter. No doubt it is a complaint letter to God. No doubt it is a list of grievances. No doubt he is writing the New Testament version of Lamentations. He has every reason to be bitter and to complain. But he isn't, and he doesn't. Instead, he writes a letter that two thousand years later is still known as a treatise on contentment.

Sound interesting? Of course it does. Who couldn't use a guide to joy in this world? Let's follow Paul as he guides us down the trail to unearthly joy and otherworldly peace.

LESSON ONE

PRAYING FOR OTHERS

MAX
LUCADO

REFLECTION

Prayer. We hear sermons about it. We talk about it. Perhaps we even read books about it. But when it comes to conversing with God, one on one, what are our actual habits? Spend a few minutes honestly pondering these questions:

- How much time do you spend in an average day actually talking to the Lord?
- What percentage of your praying is devoted to: (a) adoring/praising God _____; (b) thanking God _____; (c) asking God to meet your physical/spiritual/relational/emotional needs _____; (d) interceding for the needs of others _____; (e) being still/listening quietly _____?
- On a scale of 1 to 10 (if 1 is "awful!" and 10 is "awesome!") how would you rate your prayer life and why?

SITUATION

From a prison in Rome, Paul writes this joy-filled epistle of encouragement. The recipients? The church he established in the Roman colony of Philippi on his second missionary journey in AD 50 (see Acts 16). Paul's deep affection for this Macedonian congregation is demonstrated by his faithfulness in prayer for them.

OBSERVATION

Read Philippians 1:3–11 from the NCV or the NKJV.

NCV

3I thank my God every time I remember you, 4always praying with joy for all of you. 5I thank God for the help you gave me while I preached the Good News—help you gave from the first day you believed until now. 6God began doing a good work in you, and I am sure he will continue it until it is finished when Jesus Christ comes again.

7And I know that I am right to think like this about all of you, because I have you in my heart. All of you share in God's grace with me while I am in prison and while I am defending and proving the truth of the Good News. 8God knows that I want to see you very much, because I love all of you with the love of Christ Jesus.

9This is my prayer for you: that your love will grow more and more; that you will have knowledge and understanding with your love; 10that you will see the difference between good and bad and will choose the good; that you will be pure and without wrong for the coming of Christ; 11that you will do many good things with the help of Christ to bring glory and praise to God.

NKJV

3I thank my God upon every remembrance of you, 4always in every prayer of mine making request for you all with joy, 5for your fellowship in the gospel from the first day until now, 6being confident of this very thing, that He who has begun a good work in you will complete it until the day of Jesus Christ; 7just as it is right for me to think this of you all, because I have you in my heart, inasmuch as both in my chains and in the defense and confirmation of the gospel, you all are partakers with me of grace. 8For God is my witness, how greatly I long for you all with the affection of Jesus Christ.

9And this I pray, that your love may abound still more and more in knowledge and all discernment, 10that you may approve the things that are excellent, that you may be sincere and without offense till the day of Christ, 11being filled with the fruits of righteousness which are by Jesus Christ, to the glory and praise of God.

EXPLORATION

1. What descriptive words and phrases does Paul use to describe his attitude in prayer?

2. What five words would you use to describe your prayer life?

3. What is the great promise for Christians in verse 6?

4. What specific requests did Paul bring before God when he prayed for the Philippians?

5. How does increasing knowledge and insight help in one's growth?

INSPIRATION

I'd like you to think about someone. His name is not important. His looks are immaterial. His gender is of no concern. His title is irrelevant. He is important not because of who he is, but because of what he did.

He went to Jesus on behalf of a friend. His friend was sick, and Jesus could help, and someone needed to go to Jesus, so someone went. Others cared for the sick man in other ways. Some brought food, others provided treatment, still others comforted the family. Each role was crucial. Each person was helpful, but none was more vital than the one who went to Jesus.

He went because he was asked to go. An earnest appeal came from the family of the afflicted. "We need someone who will tell Jesus that my brother is sick. We need someone to ask him to come. Will you go?"

The question came from two sisters. They would have gone themselves, but they couldn't leave their brother's bedside. They needed someone else to go for them. Not just anyone, mind you, for not just anyone could. Some were too busy, others didn't know the way. Some fatigued too quickly, others were inexperienced on the path. Not everyone could go.

And not everyone would go. This was no small request the sisters were making. They needed a diligent ambassador, someone who knew how to find Jesus. Someone who wouldn't quit mid-journey. Someone who would make sure the message was delivered. Someone who was as convinced as they were that Jesus *must* know what had happened.

They knew of a trustworthy person, and to that person they went. They entrusted their needs to someone, and that someone took those needs to Christ.

"So Mary and Martha sent *someone* to tell Jesus, 'Lord, the one you love is sick'" (John 11:3 NCV, emphasis mine).

Someone carried the request. Someone walked the trail. Someone went to Jesus on behalf of Lazarus. And because someone went, Jesus responded. (From *The Great House of God* by Max Lucado)

REACTION

6. How reliable or faithful are you to pray for others when they request such spiritual support?

7. If you were to receive an inspired letter from the apostle Paul today, which of your qualities or habits would he praise?

8. In what specific area of your life do you need to claim the promise of 1:6?

9. When it comes to spiritual insight and discernment, how solid are you?

10. What elements from Paul's example of prayer here do you need to incorporate in your own life?

11. To what Christian friend or relative can you write a short note or e-mail today for the purpose of providing spiritual encouragement?

LIFE LESSONS

Someone has observed that joy is found in focusing on Jesus first, Others second, and yourself last. Since these were Paul's priorities, it's no mystery how he could write such an upbeat epistle even when he found himself incarcerated! Philippians begins with an excited, Christ-centered description of Paul's habits of intercession. As he talked to the Lord about his Macedonian friends, he not only remembered their past acts of love with thanksgiving, but he also requested heavenly wisdom for their worldly struggles. Furthermore, Paul looked ahead confidently to their certain maturity. Paul prayed constantly (1 Thess. 5:17). He prayed with faith. And, he assured them of his spiritual support. The result was a contagious joy, for them and for him. Prayer proves the psalmist's claim, "Being with you will fill me with joy" (Ps. 16:11 NCV).

DEVOTION

Father, thank you for the reminder that I can pray for others no matter where I am, no matter what my circumstances. Help me develop a more consistent ministry of interceding for my family members, friends, coworkers, and neighbors. Give me joy as I pray—and let me always see prayer as a privilege and not a duty.

For more Bible passages on intercessory prayer, see Numbers 14:1–24; Nehemiah 1:1–10; and Ephesians 1:15–23; 3:14–21.

To complete the book of Philippians during this twelve-part study, read Philippians 1:1–11.

JOURNALING

List some specific areas of spiritual growth you'd like to see God make in your family members. As you do, pray for God to bring about these changes in his way and his timing.

TRIUMPH IN TROUBLE

MAX
LUCADO

REFLECTION

Control is a big deal to most folks. Whether mentally or manually (using tools like a Day-Timer or a PDA), most of us devise daily "to do" lists and weekly agendas. How do you typically respond when life doesn't cooperate with your plans?

SITUATION

Even when he was stuck in a Roman prison, the vigorous, active, always-on-the-go apostle Paul saw evidence of God's control and wisdom. He reminds us that in the hard (and hard-to-understand) moments of life, God is at work, orchestrating events and bringing about his perfect will.

OBSERVATION

Read Philippians 1:12–18 from the NCV or the NKJV.

NCV

12I want you brothers and sisters to know that what has happened to me has helped to spread the Good News. 13All the palace guards and everyone else knows that I am in prison because I am a believer in Christ. 14Because I am in prison, most of the believers have become more bold in Christ and are not afraid to speak the word of God.

15It is true that some preach about Christ because they are jealous and ambitious, but others preach about Christ because they want to help. 16They preach because they have love, and they know that God gave me the work of defending the Good News. 17But the others preach about Christ for selfish and wrong reasons, wanting to make trouble for me in prison.

18But it doesn't matter. The important thing is that in every way, whether for right or wrong reasons, they are preaching about Christ. So I am happy, and I will continue to be happy.

NKJV

12But I want you to know, brethren, that the things which happened to me have actually turned out for the furtherance of the gospel, 13so that it has become evident to the whole palace guard, and to all the rest, that my chains are in Christ; 14and most of the brethren in the Lord, having become confident by my chains, are much more bold to speak the word without fear.

15Some indeed preach Christ even from envy and strife, and some also from good will: 16The former preach Christ from selfish ambition, not sincerely, supposing to add affliction to my chains; 17but the latter out of love, knowing that I am appointed for the defense of the gospel. 18What then? Only that in every way, whether in pretense or in truth, Christ is preached; and in this I rejoice, yes, and will rejoice.

EXPLORATION

1. Paul was a man of action—a missionary church planter. How hard do you think it was for him to adjust to life behind bars (or at least in chains when under house arrest)?

2. How did Paul turn his bad circumstances into a positive situation?

3. What was the effect of Paul's imprisonment on other believers?

4. Paul refused to dwell on the negative aspects of things. How does one develop this habit?

5. What bad situations are present in your life right now?

INSPIRATION

Scripture, from Old Testament to New, from prophets to poets to preachers, renders one unanimous chorus: God directs the affairs of humanity. As Paul wrote, *"God . . . is the blessed controller of all things, the king over all kings and the master of all masters"* (I Tim. 6:15 PHILLIPS, emphasis mine).

No leaf falls without God's knowledge. No dolphin gives birth without his permission. No wave crashes on the shore apart from his calculation. God has never been surprised. Not once . . .

Denying the sovereignty of God requires busy scissors and results in a hole-y Bible, for many holes are made as the verses are cut out. Amazingly, some people opt to extract such passages. Unable to reconcile human suffering with absolute sovereignty, they dilute God's Word. Rabbi Kushner did.

His book *When Bad Things Happen to Good People* reached a disturbing conclusion: God can't run the world. Kushner suggested that Job, the most famous sufferer, was "forced to choose between a good God who is not totally powerful, or a powerful God who is not totally good."

The rabbi speaks for many. *God is strong. Or God is good. But God is not both.* Else, how do you explain birth defects, coast-crashing hurricanes, AIDS, or the genocide of the Tutsi in the 1990s? If God cares, he isn't strong; if he is strong, he doesn't care. He can't be both.

But according to the Bible, he is exactly that. Furthermore, according to the Bible, the problem is not the strength or kindness of God. The problem is the agenda of the human race. We pursue the wrong priority. We want good health, a good income, a good night's rest, and a good retirement. Our priority is *We*.

God's priority, however, is God. (From *Come Thirsty* by Max Lucado)

REACTION

6. How *do* we reconcile the power and goodness of God with natural disasters and man-made evil?

7. How might God be wanting to work through the bad situations in your life just now—the ones you listed earlier— for his glory and your good?

8. Almost as an aside, Paul gives us a good principle in this passage about the possible wrong motives of others. What is the principle?

9. What are some common wrong motives that Christians have for praying, witnessing, attending worship, etc.?

10. Paul was passionate about the advance of the gospel. What would those who know you best say is your driving desire in life?

11. How much of an encouragement to others is your normal response to difficulty?

LIFE LESSONS

Let's be honest. *Control* is an illusion. We can't engineer problem-free events, and we can't make people live the way we want them to live. About the only thing we can control is our own response to life situations. Will we look for God in the midst of trouble? Will we trust that he is at work? Will we keep doing right no matter what? Will we choose to remain positive? Paul is a great role model for us. He absolutely refused to pursue his own agenda, because he saw himself as a mere servant of Christ. He made plans, but he held them in an open hand. When hard times came, his response wasn't to pout. It was to yield to God's authority by humbly saying, "Thy will be done."

DEVOTION

Lord, I realize that oftentimes I am guilty of desiring my will more than yours. As a result I get frustrated and foul when things don't go according to my plans. Teach me the art of surrendering to your bigger and better purposes. Show me how to experience triumph even in times of trouble.

For more Bible passages on triumph through trouble, see Genesis 45:1–13; 50:15–21; Isaiah 14:27; 55:8–9; Daniel 3; and Luke 23:32–24:8.

To complete the book of Philippians during this twelve-part study, read Philippians 1:12–26.

JOURNALING

Review a past trial or hardship and list some positives that came from that experience.

STANDING FIRM

MAX LUCADO

REFLECTION

There's never been a time in the last two thousand years when Christians haven't been ridiculed and criticized by the people of the world. What are some of the most common complaints against believers, and which of these attacks (if any) have legitimacy?

SITUATION

Writing from a Roman prison to the church at Philippi, Paul expresses his joyous confidence that, despite life's hardships, God remains in control. In this paragraph, he urges the Philippian Christians to live with a steadfast unity that will attract others to the gospel.

OBSERVATION

Read Philippians 1:27–30 from the NCV or the NKJV.

NCV

²⁷Only one thing concerns me: Be sure that you live in a way that brings honor to the Good News of Christ. Then whether I come and visit you or am away from you, I will hear that you are standing strong with one purpose, that you work together as one for the faith of the Good News, ²⁸and that you are not afraid of those who are against you. All of this is proof that your enemies will be destroyed but that you will be saved by God. ²⁹God gave you the honor not only of believing in Christ but also of suffering for him, both of which bring glory to Christ. ³⁰When I was with you, you saw the struggles I had, and you hear about the struggles I am having now. You yourselves are having the same kind of struggles.

NKJV

²⁷Only let your conduct be worthy of the gospel of Christ, so that whether I come and see you or am absent, I may hear of your affairs, that you stand fast in one spirit, with one mind striving together for the faith of the gospel, ²⁸and not in any way terrified by your adversaries, which is to them a proof of perdition, but to you of salvation, and that from God. ²⁹For to you it has been granted on behalf of Christ, not only to believe in Him, but also to suffer for His sake, ³⁰having the same conflict which you saw in me and now hear is in me.

EXPLORATION

1. What are some actions that are unworthy of Christ—that dishonor his name in the eyes of the world?

2. Why is it so hard for churches to stand "strong with one purpose" (v. 27 NCV)?

3. Paul's only real concern for the Philippians was an apparent lack of unity. What factors pose the most dangerous threat to the harmony of a local church?

4. According to Paul, what behavior contributes to fearlessness among believers?

5. Why is suffering such a common topic in the New Testament and such a rare reality in the lives of modern, Western Christians?

INSPIRATION

This phrase is a petition, not a proclamation. A request, not an announcement. Hallowed *be* your name . . . Do whatever it takes to be holy in my life. Take your rightful place on the throne. Exalt yourself. Magnify yourself. Glorify yourself. You be Lord, and I'll be quiet.

The word *hallowed* comes from the word *holy,* and the word *holy* means "to sepa-rate." The ancestry of the term can be traced back to an ancient word which means "to cut." To be holy, then, is to be a cut above the norm, superior, extra-ordinary. Remember . . . the Holy One dwells on a different level from the rest of us. What frightens us does not frighten him. What troubles us does not trouble him.

I'm more a landlubber than a sailor, but I've puttered around in a bass boat enough to know the secret for finding land in a storm . . . You don't aim at another boat. You certainly don't stare at the waves. You set your sights on an object unaffected by the wind—a light on the shore—and go straight toward it. The light is unaffected by the storm.

By seeking God . . . you do the same. When you set your sights on our God, you focus on the one "a cut above" any storm life may bring. (From *The Great House of God* by Max Lucado)

REACTION

6. Since God is holy, how does your behavior as a citizen of his kingdom need to be modified so it reflects his character?

7. What keeps you from wholeheartedly praying, "Do whatever it takes to be holy in my life"?

8. What precise role does the Holy Spirit play in helping preserve unity among God's people?

9. Paul alludes to the reality that people will notice and discuss the behavior of believers (see verse 27). What is your reputation as a Christian? What about your church's?

10. Paul challenged the Philippians to strive "together for the faith of the gospel" (v. 27 NKJV). What would this look like (specifically and practically) in the life of your church or small group?

11. When have you struggled or suffered most as a Christian?

LIFE LESSONS

As Jesus' earthly life and ministry drew to a close, he spoke urgently and prayed fervently about the unified way his followers should live. In short, Christ wants us living in harmony (John 17) and loving one another sacrificially (John 13:34–35). Such unconditional devotion sets us apart and causes the world to stare in awe. Conversely, when Christians bicker and feud, when churches split, we bring shame on the name of Christ, and the world mocks. It is only in unity that we shine, only together that we fully enjoy all the blessings of God. Shared sorrows are halved sorrows. Shared joys are doubled joys. What will you change this week to ensure that all your interactions with other believers are worthy of the gospel?

DEVOTION

Lord Jesus, because you deserve to be represented by believers who are holy and who live in harmony with one another, I make the psalmist's prayer my own: "LORD, try me and test me; look closely into my heart and mind" (Ps. 26:2 NCV). Show me any actions I need to change.

For more Bible passages on conduct worthy of Christ, see 1 Corinthians 1:10; 2 Corinthians 13:11; 1 Timothy 4:12; James 3:13; 1 Peter 2:12; and 2 Peter 3:11.

To complete the book of Philippians during this twelve-part study, read Philippians 1:27–30.

JOURNALING

What damaged relationship do you have with another Christian that needs attention, and what will it take on your part to heal the rift?

LESSON FOUR

ALL FOR ONE

MAX
LUCADO

REFLECTION

Perhaps you've been fortunate to be part of a sports team, fraternal organization, congregation or small group marked by unusual camaraderie and a deep sense of oneness. Or, on the opposite end of the spectrum, maybe you've witnessed the painful breakup of a marriage, company, or church. Take a few minutes to jot your memories of one of those vivid situations.

SITUATION

Philippians is essentially a thank-you note, with the apostle Paul expressing gratitude for a generous financial gift sent by a church he founded in Macedonia in about AD 51. However, Paul uses this short letter to also challenge the Christians at Philippi to settle their minor differences and live in unity before a watching world.

OBSERVATION

Read Philippians 2:1–4 from the NCV or the NKJV.

NCV

¹Does your life in Christ give you strength? Does his love comfort you? Do we share together in the spirit? Do you have mercy and kindness? ²If so, make me very happy by having the same thoughts, sharing the same love, and having one mind and purpose. ³When you do things, do not let selfishness or pride be your guide. Instead, be humble and give more honor to others than to yourselves. ⁴Do not be interested only in your own life, but be interested in the lives of others.

NKJV

¹Therefore if there is any consolation in Christ, if any comfort of love, if any fellowship of the Spirit, if any affection and mercy, ²fulfill my joy by being like-minded, having the same love, being of one accord, of one mind. ³Let nothing be done through selfish ambition or conceit, but in lowliness of mind let each esteem others better than himself. ⁴Let each of you look out not only for his own interests, but also for the interests of others.

EXPLORATION

1. Scholars point out that the "if" statements in 2:1 in the NKJV should really be translated "since." In other words Christians *do* enjoy these advantages. Why are these such important privileges?

2. What are the implications of the Bible's claim that the same Spirit of God indwells all believers?

3. How would you define or describe in everyday terms what the Bible means by "being like-minded . . . being of one accord, of one mind" (v. 2 NKJV)? Give some examples.

4. How can a Christian tell if he or she is being motivated by "selfish ambition or conceit" (v. 3 NKJV)?

5. Why is it so hard to put the needs and interests of others above one's own?

INSPIRATION

Broken people come to churches. Not with broken bones, but broken hearts, homes, dreams, and lives. They limp in on fractured faith, and if the church operates as the church, they find healing. Pastor-teachers touch and teach. Gospel bearers share good news. Prophets speak words of truth. Visionaries dream of greater impact. Some administer. Some pray. Some lead. Some follow. But all help to heal brokenness: "to make the body of Christ stronger."

My favorite example of this truth involves an elder in our church, Randy Boggs. He loves the congregation so much he smells like the sheep he tends. Between running a business and raising a family, he encourages the sick and calls on the confused. Few men have kinder hearts. And yet, few men have had their hearts put on ice as his was the night his father was murdered and his stepmother was arrested for his death. She was eventually acquitted, but the deed left Randy with no dad, no inheritance, and no answers.

How do you recover from that? Randy will tell you; through the church. Friends prayed for him, wept with him, stood by him. Finally, after months of wrestling with anger and sorrow, he resolved to move on. The decision came in a moment of worship. God sutured Randy's heart with the lyrics of a hymn. Randy calls it a miracle. That makes two of us.

God heals his family through his family. In the church we use our gifts to love each other, honor one another, keep an eye on troublemakers, and carry each other's burdens. Do you need encouragement, prayers, or a hospitable home? God entrusts the church to purvey these treasures. Consider the church God's treatment center . . . Don't miss it. No one is strong all the time. Don't miss the place to find your place and heal your hurts. (From *Cure for the Common Life* by Max Lucado)

REACTION

6. How much healing is likely to take place in a church where a majority of the people are looking out for number one?

7. One of the great claims of the New Testament is that we are "in Christ." The phrase occurs eight times in Philippians alone. How should we act as members of his body (see 1 Corinthians 12)?

8. Our culture practically worships the ideals of autonomy and individualism. In what ways are these values counterproductive to what God is trying to do in and through his body?

9. What exactly is "lowliness of mind" (v. 3 NKJV)?

10. List some practical ways that Christians can demonstrate humility and give more honor to others than to themselves.

11. Since we are naturally self-centered, how do we develop the kind of mind-set that looks first to the needs and interests of others?

LIFE LESSONS

Like it or not, we are walking billboards for the gospel. People form opinions about Christ and draw conclusions about our faith based on how we live and interact. Imagine the damage when Christians claim to be brand-new people but then hold on to petty grudges. Or when we advertise ourselves as a God-inhabited community, yet our relationships are marked by self-centeredness and divisiveness. Paul suggests that such disunity is the result of spiritual immaturity and insecurity. It's only when we truly embrace the infinite resources provided by Christ (2:1) that we find the capacity to stop our selfish grasping for lesser things. When secure in him, we are freed up to become others-centered. Such selflessness shocks the world.

DEVOTION

Father, you have given us all we need to be a jaw-dropping faith community. We are in Christ. We experience the comfort and force of his love. We share life in the Spirit who fills us with mercy and kindness. Now, strengthened by and secure in all these resources, may we let go of our selfish desires and pursue lives of radical servanthood.

For more Bible passages on unity, see Romans 12:5; 1 Corinthians 10:17; Galatians 3:28; Ephesians 4:3; and 1 Peter 3:8.

To complete the book of Philippians during this twelve-part study, read Philippians 2:1–4.

JOURNALING

Here are the interests of five significant people in my life and some specific ideas for selflessly putting their needs first this week . . .

LESSON FIVE

ULTIMATE
SERVANTHOOD

MAX
LUCADO

REFLECTION

Think back on the various jobs you've had, all the volunteer assignments that you have undertaken. What assignments or responsibilities have been the most menial and humbling? Describe one such experience.

SITUATION

For a young church beginning to struggle with conflict and facing the growing threat of persecution, Paul points to the ultimate example of humble servant-hood—the incarnation of Christ. He is our model of humility and service. Only in him, and only by embracing his attitudes and actions, do we find true unity and joy.

OBSERVATION

Read Philippians 2:5–11 from the NCV or the NKJV.

NCV

⁵*In your lives you must think and act like Christ Jesus.*

⁶*Christ himself was like God in everything.*

But he did not think that being equal with God was something to be used for his own benefit.

⁷*But he gave up his place with God and made himself nothing.*

He was born to be a man

and became like a servant.

⁸*And when he was living as a man,*

he humbled himself and was fully obedient to God,

even when that caused his death—death on a cross.

⁹*So God raised him to the highest place.*

God made his name greater than every other name

¹⁰*so that every knee will bow to the name of Jesus—*

everyone in heaven, on earth, and under the earth.

¹¹*And everyone will confess that Jesus Christ is Lord*

and bring glory to God the Father.

NKJV

⁵*Let this mind be in you which was also in Christ Jesus, ⁶who, being in the form of God, did not consider it robbery to be equal with God, ⁷but made Himself of no reputation, taking the form of a bondservant, and coming in the likeness of men. ⁸And being found in appearance as a man, He humbled Himself and became obedient to the point of death, even the death of the cross. ⁹Therefore God also has highly exalted Him and given Him the name which is above every name, ¹⁰that at the name of Jesus every knee should bow, of those in heaven, and of those on earth, and of those under the earth, ¹¹and that every tongue should confess that Jesus Christ is Lord, to the glory of God the Father.*

EXPLORATION

1. Being a disciple means imitating one's master or teacher in thoughts, actions, and character. Where are your attitudes unlike Christ's?

2. Verses 6–7 note how Christ, in taking on full humanity, resolved not to cling to his divine prerogatives, but "made Himself of no reputation" (NKJV). Can you cite some specific examples of this from the Gospels?

3. As God's ultimate servant, Christ always acted in absolute dependence on his Father (Luke 4:14; John 5:19; 8:28; 14:10). What can we learn from this example?

4. Christ devoted his entire life to serving others. Not once did he live for "his own benefit" (v. 6 NCV). If we dare to live likewise, how can we be sure our needs will be met?

5. How does God reward those who humble themselves and serve (see Luke 18:14)?

INSPIRATION

Jesus came to serve. He selected prayer over sleep, the wilderness over the Jordan, irascible apostles over obedient angels. I'd have gone with the angels. Given the choice, I would have built my apostle team out of cherubim and seraphim or Gabriel and Michael, eyewitnesses of Red Sea rescues and Mount Carmel falling fires. I'd choose the angels.

Not Jesus. He picked the people. Peter, Andrew, John, and Matthew. When they feared the storm, he stilled it. When they had no coin for taxes, he supplied it. And when they had no wine for the wedding or food for the multitude, he made both.

He came to serve.

He let a woman in Samaria interrupt his rest, a woman in adultery interrupt his sermon, a woman with a disease interrupt his plans, and one with remorse interrupt his meal.

Though none of the apostles washed his feet, he washed theirs. Though none of the soldiers at the cross begged for mercy, he extended it. And though his followers skedaddled like scared rabbits on Thursday, he came searching for them on Easter Sunday. The resurrected King ascended to heaven only after he'd spent forty days with his friends—teaching them, encouraging them . . . serving them.

Why? It's what he came to do. He came to serve . . .

Let's follow his example. Let's "put on the apron of humility, to serve one another" (1 Pet. 5:5 TEV). Jesus entered the world to serve. We can enter our jobs, our homes, our churches. Servanthood requires no unique skill or seminary degree. (From *Cure for the Common Life* by Max Lucado)

REACTION

6. If servanthood requires no special training or gifting, why is it so rare?

7. What are the key ingredients to a life of servanthood?

8. What would the atmosphere be like in a church filled with humble servants?

9. Jesus wasn't after prestige or honor or authority. Why are so many of his followers so hungry and desperate for these things?

10. What is it like to work for you or to be under your authority? How do you treat those who serve under you?

11. Servanthood—giving up one's rights, putting others first, refusing to promote oneself—how can such a humble lifestyle be the path to glory and joy?

LIFE LESSONS

Think of this: If the Father in heaven is not only with us, but in us, if he never abandons us, if he listens to us and cares about us and wants only the best for us, then all things are possible. We no longer have to scramble around trying to make life work. We can relax. We can go "off-duty." We can let go of the draining, joy-depleting habit of looking out for number one. Even better than that, when we are convinced that the Father is absolutely for us, we are freed up to focus all our attention and energy and efforts on living for him by serving others. As surrendered servants, we can rest assured he will meet all our needs.

DEVOTION

Lord Jesus, I thank you for your humble sacrifice. You gave your life to give me life. In gratitude, let me respond today by giving my life to serve others. Thank you for the assurance that you will supply all my needs.

For more Bible passages on humble servanthood, see Micah 6:8; Matthew 20:28; Luke 14:10; 22:26–27; John 13:1–17; James 4:10; and 1 Peter 5:5.

To complete the book of Philippians during this twelve-part study, read Philippians 2:5–11.

JOURNALING

Living and serving by faith isn't a series of grandiose actions. It is trusting God in small things as a way of life. For example, spending thirty minutes with a neighbor when I really had intended to balance the checkbook, or being a chaperone on the youth retreat when I really wanted a leisurely weekend at home. List some tangible acts of servanthood that you could engage in this week . . .

L E S S O N   S I X

SHINING
FOR CHRIST

MAX
LUCADO

REFLECTION

Like snowflakes and fingerprints, no two Christians are alike. God is working in our lives in varied ways and according to a unique blueprint. What are the areas of your life in which you see tangible growth and progress, and what are the areas in which you long for change?

SITUATION

Imprisoned because of his fearless faith, the apostle Paul sends this encouraging and challenging letter to the Christians in Philippi. His charge? Look at the example of Jesus and live humbly. Yield to God's working in your lives. As we do these things, Christians "shine like stars in the dark world" (v. 15 NCV).

OBSERVATION

Read Philippians 2:12–18 from the NCV or the NKJV.

NCV

12My dear friends, you have always obeyed God when I was with you. It is even more important that you obey now while I am away from you. Keep on working to complete your salvation with fear and trembling, 13because God is working in you to help you want to do and be able to do what pleases him.

14Do everything without complaining or arguing. 15Then you will be innocent and without any wrong. You will be God's children without fault. But you are living with crooked and mean people all around you, among whom you shine like stars in the dark world. 16You offer the teaching that gives life. So when Christ comes again, I can be happy because my work was not wasted. I ran the race and won.

¹⁷*Your faith makes you offer your lives as a sacrifice in serving God. If I have to offer my own blood with your sacrifice, I will be happy and full of joy with all of you.* ¹⁸*You also should be happy and full of joy with me.*

NKJV

¹²*Therefore, my beloved, as you have always obeyed, not as in my presence only, but now much more in my absence, work out your own salvation with fear and trembling;* ¹³*for it is God who works in you both to will and to do for His good pleasure.*

¹⁴*Do all things without complaining and disputing,* ¹⁵*that you may become blameless and harmless, children of God without fault in the midst of a crooked and perverse generation, among whom you shine as lights in the world,* ¹⁶*holding fast the word of life, so that I may rejoice in the day of Christ that I have not run in vain or labored in vain.*

¹⁷*Yes, and if I am being poured out as a drink offering on the sacrifice and service of your faith, I am glad and rejoice with you all.* ¹⁸*For the same reason you also be glad and rejoice with me.*

EXPLORATION

1. Go through this brief passage and underline all the verbs. Note what Paul says God is doing. Observe the actions expected of believers. What strikes you?

2. There is a common tendency for young Christians to rely heavily on the faith and presence of other believers (see verse 12). When does spiritual dependence become unhealthy?

3. What's the crucial difference between working out your own salvation (see verse 12 NKJV) and the attempt by many to work *for* one's salvation?

4. How can Christians live with joy if we also are expected to live "with fear and trembling" (see verse 12 NJKV)?

5. How do we avoid the ever-present danger of trying to live exemplary lives so that *we* will get the attention and admiration of others?

INSPIRATION

We applause-aholics have done it all: dropped names, sung loudly, dressed up to look classy, dressed down to look cool, quoted authors we've never read, spouted Greek we've never studied. For the life of me, I believe Satan trains battalions of demons to whisper one question in our ears: "What are people thinking of you?"

A deadly query. What they think of us matters not. What they think of God matters all. God will not share his glory with another (Isa. 42:8). Next time you need a nudge away from the spotlight, remember: *You are simply one link in a chain, an unimportant link at that.*

Don't agree? Take it up with the apostle. *"So the one who plants is not important, and the one who waters is not important. Only God, who makes things grow, is important"* (1 Cor. 3:7 NCV, emphasis mine).

Remember the other messengers God has used?

A donkey to speak to Balaam (Num. 22:28).

A staff-turned-snake to stir Pharaoh (Exod. 7:10).

He used stubborn oxen to make a point about reverence and a big fish to make a point about reluctant preachers (1 Sam. 6:1–12; Jonah 1:1–17).

God doesn't need you and me to do his work. We are expedient messengers, ambassadors by his kindness, not by our cleverness.

It's not about us, and it angers him when we think it is. (From *It's Not About Me* by Max Lucado)

REACTION

6. What are some signs that we have crossed the line from thinking, *What are people thinking of my Savior?* to, *What are people thinking about me?*

7. What exactly would working out "your own salvation with fear and trembling" (v. 12 NKJV) look like in your life this week?

8. What are some of the ways "God is working in you to help you want to do and be able to do what pleases him" (v. 13 NCV)?

9. How much of a problem do you have with complaining or arguing?

10. What are some godly qualities or actions that would result in your shining more brightly for Christ?

11. Propose some practical ways you can "hold fast the word of life" (see verse 16 NKJV)—both clinging to it, and offering it to others?

LIFE LESSONS

What does the moon do? She generates no light. Contrary to the lyrics of the song, this harvest moon cannot shine on. Apart from the sun, the moon is nothing more than a gray, pockmarked rock. But properly positioned, the moon beams. Let her do what she was made to do, and a clod of dirt becomes a source of inspiration and a symbol of romance. The moon reflects the greater light. What would happen if we accepted our place as Son reflectors? What if we made it our goal to shine with all the brightness of Christ?

DEVOTION

Lord, I want to make progress in the faith, not so people will notice me, but so that people might marvel at you. I offer you my will—make it yours. I offer my weakness and request your infinite strength. Shine through me today.

For more Bible passages on shining for Christ, see Judges 5:31; Psalm 34:5; Daniel 12:3; Matthew 5:14–16; John 5:35; Acts 6:15; 13:47; 2 Corinthians 3:18; and Ephesians 5:8.

To complete the book of Philippians during this twelve-part study, read Philippians 2:12–18.

JOURNALING

"Fear and trembling" suggests a deep reverence for God. How does one develop this sense of holy awe?

ROLE
MODELS

MAX
LUCADO

REFLECTION

Our culture has its share of celebrities, and oftentimes these people are famous . . . for nothing more than being famous! There is, of course, a huge difference between being a character and having character. Who are the people you most admire—especially in the spiritual realm—and why?

SITUATION

Having pointed the Philippian Christians to Jesus as the ultimate example of humble servanthood, Paul now mentions two of his colleagues in ministry: Timothy and Epaphroditus. Their character and conduct serve as role models of faithfulness and selflessness.

OBSERVATION

Read Philippians 2:19–30 from the NCV or the NKJV.

NCV

¹⁹I hope in the Lord Jesus to send Timothy to you soon. I will be happy to learn how you are. ²⁰I have no one else like Timothy, who truly cares for you. ²¹Other people are interested only in their own lives, not in the work of Jesus Christ. ²²You know the kind of person Timothy is. You know he has served with me in telling the Good News, as a son serves his father. ²³I plan to send him to you quickly when I know what will happen to me. ²⁴I am sure that the Lord will help me to come to you soon.

²⁵Epaphroditus, my brother in Christ, works and serves with me in the army of Christ. When I needed help, you sent him to me. I think now that I must send him back to you, ²⁶because he wants very much to see all of you. He is worried because you heard that he was sick. ²⁷Yes, he was sick, and nearly died, but God had mercy on him and me too so that I would not have more sadness. ²⁸I want very much to send him to you so that when you see him you can be happy, and I can stop worrying about you. ²⁹Welcome him in the Lord with much joy. Give honor to people like him, ³⁰because he almost died for the work of Christ. He risked his life to give me the help you could not give in your service to me.

NKJV

¹⁹But I trust in the Lord Jesus to send Timothy to you shortly, that I also may be encouraged when I know your state. ²⁰For I have no one like-minded, who will sincerely care for your state. ²¹For all seek their own, not the things which are of Christ Jesus. ²²But you know his proven character, that as a son with his father he served with me in the gospel. ²³Therefore I hope to send him at once, as soon as I see how it goes with me. ²⁴But I trust in the Lord that I myself shall also come shortly.

²⁵Yet I considered it necessary to send to you Epaphroditus, my brother, fellow worker, and fellow soldier, but your messenger and the one who ministered to my need; ²⁶since he was longing for you all, and was distressed because you had heard that he was sick. ²⁷For indeed he was sick almost unto death; but God had mercy on him, and not only on him but on me also, lest I should have sorrow upon sorrow. ²⁸Therefore I sent him the more eagerly, that when you see him again you may rejoice, and I may be less sorrowful. ²⁹Receive him therefore in the Lord with all gladness, and hold such men in esteem; ³⁰because for the work of Christ he came close to death, not regarding his life, to supply what was lacking in your service toward me.

EXPLORATION

1. Why did Paul hold Timothy in such high regard?

2. What were the outstanding qualities of Epaphroditus?

3. From what you see in the text, would you enjoy being in a small group more with Timothy or Epaphroditus? Why?

4. Paul encouraged the Philippians to honor or esteem people like Epaphroditus. What does this look like?

5. We tend to place the people mentioned in Scripture on a pedestal. Why is this a disservice to them and to us?

INSPIRATION

The church of Jesus Christ began with a group of frightened men in a second-floor room in Jerusalem.

Though trained and taught, they didn't know what to say. Though they'd marched with him for three years, they now sat . . . afraid. They were timid soldiers, reluctant warriors, speechless messengers.

Their most courageous act was to get up and lock the door.

Some looked out the window, some looked at the wall, some looked at the floor, but all looked inside themselves.

And well they should, for it was an hour of self-examination. All their efforts seemed so futile. Nagging their memories were the promises they'd made but not kept. When the Roman soldiers took Jesus, Jesus' followers took off. With the very wine of the covenant on their breath and the bread of his sacrifice in their bellies, they fled.

All those boasts of bravado? All those declarations of devotion? They lay broken and shattered at the gate of Gethsemane's garden.

We don't know where the disciples went when they fled the garden, but we do know what they took: a memory. They took a heart-stopping memory of a man who called himself no less than God in the flesh. And they couldn't get him out of their minds. Try as they might to lose him in the crowd, they couldn't forget him. If they saw a leper, they thought of his compassion. If they heard a storm, they would remember the day he silenced one. If they saw a child, they would think of the day he held one. And if they saw a lamb being carried to the temple, they would remember his face streaked with blood and his eyes flooded with love.

No, they couldn't forget him. As a result, they came back. And, as a result, the church of our Lord began with a group of frightened men in an upper room.

Sound familiar? Things haven't changed much in two thousand years, have they? How many churches today find themselves paralyzed in the upper room? (From *Six Hours One Friday* by Max Lucado)

REACTION

6. How does it encourage you to realize that the "great saints" of Scripture were fallible and fearful and sometimes fickle and faithless?

7. How does it challenge you to watch ordinary guys like Timothy and Epaphroditus live extraordinary lives of sacrifice and courage?

8. How can we, like Timothy, develop the godly quality of not being "interested only in [our] own lives" (v. 21 NCV)?

9. If your spiritual leaders were to describe you, what words and phrases would they use?

10. Epaphroditus "risked his life" to serve the Philippians. What are some lesser, but still important, risks you can take this week?

11. List three specific ways you will demonstrate humility and service to other believers today or tomorrow.

LIFE LESSONS

Dependable people are like diamonds. They are precious because they are so rare. Experience and know-how are great assets, but they're not much good without trustworthiness. Talent is wonderful, but by itself, it's not enough. Far better to be a faithful Christian. Are you? Like Timothy and Epaphroditus, are you a role model for others? Determine to be a person others can rely on. Keep your word. Show up. Be consistent. Live for others. Take risks. Be a "go to" guy or gal. Make it your goal, by God's grace, to exemplify a life of spiritual steadiness.

DEVOTION

Father, you have surrounded me with men and women who love you and who model what it means to walk with you. I praise you for the wonderful examples of godliness I have been given. Show me creative ways to honor my spiritual mentors. And work in my heart so that more and more I become that kind of role model for others.

For more Bible passages on spiritual role models, see John 13:15; 1 Corinthians 11:1; Philippians 3:17; 2 Thessalonians 3:7; 1 Timothy 4:12; and Titus 2:7.

To complete the book of Philippians during this twelve-part study, read Philippians 2:19–30.

JOURNALING

Instead of writing your thoughts here, take a few minutes to write a letter of appreciation and encouragement to someone who has been a hero and inspiration in your life.

RIGHT STANDING WITH GOD

MAX
LUCADO

REFLECTION

Every job seeker or college applicant has had the occasion to put together a résumé. Take a few minutes to compose a brief *spiritual* résumé. Don't be bashful. List your spiritual gifts, and your God-given abilities. Jot down some of your most meaningful spiritual experiences. Summarize your goals and objectives.

SITUATION

Using his own background as an example, Paul reminded the believers at Philippi of the centrality and supremacy of Christ. A right relationship with God is possible, not on the basis of what we do, but on the basis of what Christ has done. We are saved by grace through faith. We live the Christian life by grace through faith.

OBSERVATION

Read Philippians 3:1–11 from the NCV or the NKJV.

NCV

¹My brothers and sisters, be full of joy in the Lord. It is no trouble for me to write the same things to you again, and it will help you to be more ready. ²Watch out for those who do evil, who are like dogs, who demand to cut the body. ³We are the ones who are truly circumcised. We worship God through his Spirit, and our pride is in Christ Jesus. We do not put trust in ourselves or anything we can do, ⁴although I might be able to put trust in myself. If anyone thinks he has a reason to trust in himself, he should know that I have greater reason for trusting in myself. ⁵I was circumcised eight days after my birth. I am from the people of Israel and the tribe of Benjamin. I am a Hebrew, and my parents were Hebrews. I had a strict view of the law, which is why I became a Pharisee. ⁶I was so enthusiastic I tried to hurt the church. No one could find fault with the way I obeyed the law of Moses. ⁷Those things were important to me, but now I think they are worth nothing because of Christ. ⁸Not only those things, but I think that all things are worth nothing compared with the greatness of knowing Christ Jesus my Lord. Because of him, I have lost all those things, and now I know they are worthless trash. This allows me to have Christ ⁹and to belong to him. Now I am right with God, not because I followed the law, but because I believed in Christ. God uses my faith to make me right with him. ¹⁰I want to know Christ and the power that raised him from the dead. I want to share in his sufferings and become like him in his death. ¹¹Then I have hope that I myself will be raised from the dead.

NKJV

¹Finally, my brethren, rejoice in the Lord. For me to write the same things to you is not tedious, but for you it is safe.

²Beware of dogs, beware of evil workers, beware of the mutilation! ³For we are the circumcision, who worship God in the Spirit, rejoice in Christ Jesus, and have no confidence in the flesh, ⁴though I also might have confidence in the flesh. If anyone else thinks he may have confidence in the flesh, I more so: ⁵circumcised the eighth day, of the stock of Israel, of the tribe of Benjamin, a Hebrew of the Hebrews; concerning the law, a Pharisee; ⁶concerning zeal, persecuting the church; concerning the righteousness which is in the law, blameless.

⁷But what things were gain to me, these I have counted loss for Christ. ⁸Yet indeed I also count all things loss for the excellence of the knowledge of Christ Jesus my Lord, for whom I have suffered the loss of all things, and count them as rubbish, that I may gain Christ ⁹and be found in Him, not having my own righteousness, which is from the law, but that which is through faith in Christ, the righteousness which is from God by faith; ¹⁰that I may know Him and the power of His resurrection, and the fellowship of His sufferings, being conformed to His death, ¹¹if, by any means, I may attain to the resurrection from the dead.

EXPLORATION

1. How does Paul indicate here that joy is a choice rather than an elusive feeling that comes and goes?

2. The so-called Judaizers shadowed the apostles and tried to get their Gentile converts to submit to the rite of circumcision and other legalistic rituals in order to be saved. Why did this bother Paul?

3. What was Paul's purpose for sharing his impressive spiritual résumé as a devout Jew? Was he trying to brag?

4. How does Paul describe the monumental change that took place in his own religious attitudes and actions?

5. What's the difference between trying to adhere to a religious system and trusting in the person of Christ? Isn't this just semantics?

INSPIRATION

Computers are legalists, impersonal pragmatists. Push a button and get a response. Learn the system and get the printout. Blow the system and get ready for a long night.

Computers are heartless creatures. Don't expect any compassion from your laptop. They don't call it a hard disk for nothing. (Even the shell is hard.)

Some folks have a computer theology when it comes to understanding God. God is the ultimate desktop. The Bible is the maintenance manual, the Holy Spirit is the floppy disk, and Jesus is the 1–800 service number.

Call it computerized Christianity. Push the right buttons, enter the right code, insert the correct data, and bingo, print out your own salvation.

It's professional religion. You do your part and the Divine Computer does his. No need to pray (after all, you control the keyboard). No emotional attachment necessary (who wants to hug circuits?). And worship? Well, worship is a lab exercise—insert the rituals and see the results.

Computerized religion. No kneeling. No weeping. No gratitude. No emotion. It's great—unless you make a mistake. Unless you err. Unless you enter the wrong data or forget to save the manuscript. Unless you're caught on the wrong side of a power surge. And then . . . tough luck, buddy, you're on your own.

Religion by computer. That's what happens when . . .

you replace the living God with a cold system;

you replace inestimable love with pro-forma budget;

you replace the ultimate sacrifice of Christ with the puny achievements of man.

When you view God as a computer and the Christian as a number-crunching, cursor-commanding, button-pusher . . . that is religion by the computer.

God hates it. It crushes his people. It contaminates his leaders. It corrupts his children. (From *And the Angels Were Silent* by Max Lucado)

REACTION

6. What has been your experience of "computerized Christianity"?

7. Paul speaks of formerly having "confidence in the flesh" (vv. 3–4 NKJV) or trusting in himself (NCV). What exactly does he mean by this phrase?

8. Because of Christ, Paul says that the things (values, practices, etc.) that previously were so important to him, he now views as "rubbish" (v. 8 NKJV) or "worthless trash" (NCV). Is this your experience too?

9. Paul's one great passion in life was to know Christ. It's easy to say this, but how does one actually practice this?

10. How can we get religious people to understand that right standing with God doesn't depend on what they do, but rather on what Christ has done on their behalf?

11. Paul not only longed for the power of Christ, but he also wanted to "share in his sufferings" (v. 10 NCV). What does this mean?

LIFE LESSONS

Remember the story Jesus told about the two men who went to the temple to pray (Luke 18:9–14)? He described the first man, a Pharisee, as praying "with himself" (NKJV). Interesting, don't you think? This proud man proceeded to rattle off all his religious achievements. It was less a prayer and more a self-congratulatory speech! Meanwhile the other man, a dishonest tax collector, stood at a distance. Broken. Very much in touch with his own unworthiness. He humbly cried out to God for mercy. And how did heaven respond? Only the tax collector left the temple on right terms with God. Here in this short story is the simple gospel. We are made right with God—not by our own efforts, but by simply relying on God's grace.

DEVOTION

Father, thank you for the powerful reminder that salvation is a free gift. We can't earn it or deserve it. We can only receive it. Like Paul, give me an all-consuming passion for Christ. In the words of the old hymn, may "the things of earth grow strangely dim, in the light of his glory and grace."

For more Bible passages on the grace and glory of Christ, see Isaiah 53:4–6; Luke 15:11–31; John 4:1–42; Romans 3:20–28; Galatians 3:1–14; Ephesians 2:8–9; and Colossians 1:13–23.

To complete the book of Philippians during this twelve-part study, read Philippians 3:1–11.

JOURNALING

How would you explain to a highly moral friend that we do not make it to heaven on the basis of living "a good life"?

LESSON NINE

ETERNAL
FOCUS

MAX
LUCADO

REFLECTION

There are some who argue that it's possible to be so "heavenly minded" that one is no earthly good. There are others, like author C. S. Lewis, who insist that those who think the most about the world to come end up doing the most in this world. Which view do you think is right, and what are your own habits and attitudes regarding heaven?

SITUATION

Meeting Christ revolutionized Paul's life. It transformed his understanding of salvation and infused him with new purpose. His new twin passions? To know Christ and make him known. His new perspective? A realization that we must use this short life to prepare for eternity.

OBSERVATION

Read Philippians 3:12–21 from the NCV or the NKJV.

NCV

¹²I do not mean that I am already as God wants me to be. I have not yet reached that goal, but I continue trying to reach it and to make it mine. Christ wants me to do that, which is the reason he made me his. ¹³Brothers and sisters, I know that I have not yet reached that goal, but there is one thing I always do. Forgetting the past and straining toward what is ahead, ¹⁴I keep trying to reach the goal and get the prize for which God called me through Christ to the life above.

¹⁵All of us who are spiritually mature should think this way, too. And if there are things you do not agree with, God will make them clear to you. ¹⁶But we should continue following the truth we already have.

¹⁷Brothers and sisters, all of you should try to follow my example and to copy those who live the way we showed you. ¹⁸Many people live like enemies of the cross of Christ. I have often told you about them, and it makes me cry to tell you about them now. ¹⁹In the end, they will be destroyed. They do whatever their bodies want, they are proud of their shameful acts, and they think only about earthly things. ²⁰But our homeland is in heaven, and we are waiting for our Savior, the Lord Jesus Christ, to come from heaven. ²¹By his power to rule all things, he will change our simple bodies and make them like his own glorious body.

NKJV

¹²Not that I have already attained, or am already perfected; but I press on, that I may lay hold of that for which Christ Jesus has also laid hold of me. ¹³Brethren, I do not count myself to have apprehended; but one thing I do, forgetting those things which are behind and reaching forward to those things which are ahead, ¹⁴I press toward the goal for the prize of the upward call of God in Christ Jesus.

¹⁵Therefore let us, as many as are mature, have this mind; and if in anything you think otherwise, God will reveal even this to you. ¹⁶Nevertheless, to the degree that we have already attained, let us walk by the same rule, let us be of the same mind.

¹⁷Brethren, join in following my example, and note those who so walk, as you have us for a pattern. ¹⁸For many walk, of whom I have told you often, and now tell you even weeping, that they are the enemies of the cross of Christ: ¹⁹whose end is destruction, whose god is their belly, and whose glory is in their shame—who set their mind on earthly things. ²⁰For our citizenship is in heaven, from which we also eagerly wait for the Savior, the Lord Jesus Christ, ²¹who will transform our lowly body that it may be conformed to His glorious body, according to the working by which He is able even to subdue all things to Himself.

EXPLORATION

1. What words and phrases does Paul use to suggest that meeting Christ is the beginning, not the end, of one's spiritual journey?

2. What does Paul teach us here about goals, motivation, and living an intentional life?

3. Why are spiritual mentors and spiritual disciplines so important?

4. What does it mean to live as an enemy of Christ?

5. It grieved Paul to see fallen people living and dying without Christ in a fallen world. On the other hand, thoughts of the world to come gave him great joy. What excites you as you anticipate eternity (see Revelation 21 and 22)?

INSPIRATION

When I was a young man, I had plenty of people to wipe away my tears. I had two big sisters who put me under their wings. I had a dozen or so aunts and uncles. I had a mother who worked nights as a nurse and days as a mother—exercising both professions with tenderness. I even had a brother three years my elder who felt sorry for me occasionally.

But when I think about someone wiping away my tears, I think about Dad. His hands were callused and tough, his fingers short and stubby. And when my father wiped away a tear, he seemed to wipe it away forever. There was something in his touch that took away more than the drop of hurt from my cheek. It also took away my fear.

John says that someday God will wipe away your tears. The same hands that stretched the heavens will touch your cheeks. The same hands that formed the mountains will caress your face. The same hands that curled in agony as the Roman spike cut through will someday cup your face and brush away your tears. Forever.

When you think of a world where there will be no reason to cry, ever, doesn't it make you want to go home?

"There will be no more death . . ." John declares (Rev. 21:4 NCV). Can you imagine it? A world with no hearses or morgues or cemeteries or tombstones? Can you imagine a world with no spades of dirt thrown on caskets? No names chiseled into marble? No funerals? No black dresses? No black wreaths?

If one of the joys of the ministry is a bride descending the church aisle, one of the griefs is a body encased in a shiny box in front of the pulpit. It's never easy to say good-bye. It's never easy to walk away. The hardest task in this world is to place a final kiss on cold lips that cannot kiss in return. The hardest thing in this world is to say good-bye.

In the next world, John says, "good-bye" will never be spoken. (From *The Applause of Heaven* by Max Lucado)

REACTION

6. Paul and the other apostles thought and spoke and wrote frequently about heaven. What are some practical ways an eternal perspective can make a huge difference in everyday life?

7. How can Christians avoid a sense of complacency in the spiritual life?

8. Why does Paul use the metaphor of a race to describe the Christian life, and what does he mean by alluding to "the prize" (v. 14)?

9. Who are some older and wiser Christians you look to as examples, and in what ways do you pattern your life after theirs?

10. How would you be different, what would you do differently, if you decided to live each day gripped by the reality that you are a citizen of heaven?

11. Paul mentions *eagerly* awaiting the return of Christ. Do you get excited by the thought of eternity with God?

LIFE LESSONS

There are so many ways to say it: "This earth is not our home." "We are only passing through." "I am bound for the Promised Land." Given the fragility and brevity of this life (James 4:14) and the certainty of the world to come (Phil. 3:20–21), how should we live today? We need spiritual leaders and mentors who will exhort us to resist the fleeting attractions of this dying world (1 John 2:15–17). We need fellow pilgrims to journey with us along the path. Do you have such people in your life? Are you a vital part of a healthy Christian community? Ask God for strong Christian influences who can keep pointing you to the things that are true.

DEVOTION

Lord, thank you for the hope of heaven. Thank you for the promise that one day you will make everything right and all things new. Help me become more and more convinced of this truth, with the result that I live with ever-increasing passion and power.

For more Bible passages about living with an eternal perspective, see Matthew 6:19–21; John 14:1–8; 2 Corinthians 4:16–18; Colossians 3:2; Hebrews 11:24–28; 12:1–3; and 1 Peter 1:4.

To complete the book of Philippians during this twelve-part study, read Philippians 3:12–21.

JOURNALING

What are your biggest questions about eternity?

LESSON TEN

THE PEACE
OF GOD

MAX
LUCADO

REFLECTION

We have financial, medical, educational, and spiritual advantages that previous generations never imagined. And we have more counselors and psychiatrists seeing more patients and writing more tranquilizer prescriptions than at any other time in the history of the world. Why do so many people (and so many Christians) lack real peace of mind?

SITUATION

As he comes near the end of his joyous letter, Paul again urges his Philippian brothers and sisters to stand firm (see 1:27). Such stability and perseverance result, Paul says, when Christians live together in unity and when they pray earnestly and continually.

OBSERVATION

Read Philippians 4:1–7 from the NCV or the NKJV.

NCV

¹*My dear brothers and sisters, I love you and want to see you. You bring me joy and make me proud of you, so stand strong in the Lord as I have told you.*

²*I ask Euodia and Syntyche to agree in the Lord. ³And I ask you, my faithful friend, to help these women. They served with me in telling the Good News, together with Clement and others who worked with me, whose names are written in the book of life.*

⁴*Be full of joy in the Lord always. I will say again, be full of joy.*

⁵*Let everyone see that you are gentle and kind. The Lord is coming soon. ⁶Do not worry about anything, but pray and ask God for everything you need, always giving thanks. ⁷And God's peace, which is so great we cannot understand it, will keep your hearts and minds in Christ Jesus.*

NKJV

¹*Therefore, my beloved and longed-for brethren, my joy and crown, so stand fast in the Lord, beloved.*

²*I implore Euodia and I implore Syntyche to be of the same mind in the Lord. ³And I urge you also, true companion, help these women who labored with me in the gospel, with Clement also, and the rest of my fellow workers, whose names are in the Book of Life.*

⁴*Rejoice in the Lord always. Again I will say, rejoice!*

⁵*Let your gentleness be known to all men. The Lord is at hand.*

⁶*Be anxious for nothing, but in everything by prayer and supplication, with thanksgiving, let your requests be made known to God; ⁷and the peace of God, which surpasses all understanding, will guard your hearts and minds through Christ Jesus.*

EXPLORATION

1. Two leading women in the church at Philippi, Euodia and Syntyche, were obviously involved in some kind of conflict. Why are disagreements so stressful and draining?

2. An unnamed person (see verse 3) was urged by Paul to help mediate the dispute between Euodia and Synteche. How skilled are you at helping resolve conflicts?

3. How can a spirit of rejoicing help combat stressful, anxious situations?

4. In what ways does a belief in the imminent return of the Lord (v. 5) help bring you peace?

5. What is Paul's inspired counsel for times of anxiety?

INSPIRATION

A good memory makes for a good heart.

It works like this. Let's say a stress stirrer comes your way. The doctor decides you need an operation. She detects a lump and thinks it best that you have it removed. So there you are, walking out of her office. You've just been handed this cup of anxiety. What are you going to do with it? You can place it in one of two pots.

You can dump your bad news in the vat of worry and pull out the spoon. Turn on the fire. Stew on it. Stir it. Mope for a while. Brood for a time. Won't be long before you'll have a delightful pot of pessimism. Some of you have been sipping from this vat for a long time. Your friends and family have asked me to tell you that the stuff you're drinking is getting to you.

How about a different idea? The pot of prayer. Before the door of the doctor's office closes, give the problem to God. "I receive your lordship. Nothing comes to me that hasn't passed through you." In addition stir in a healthy helping of gratitude. You don't think about a lion and bear, but you do remember the tax refund, the timely counsel, or the sudden open seat on the overbooked flight. A glimpse into the past generates strength for the future.

Your part is prayer and gratitude. God's part? Peace and protection. (From *Come Thirsty* by Max Lucado)

REACTION

6. When and how have you experienced that truth: that a glimpse of the past generates strength for the future?

7. What stresses you more—being in a conflict, or having to referee a conflict between others?

8. How does a spirit of gentleness help defuse tension?

9. How would you define or describe what the Bible means by the phrase "the peace of God" (v. 7 NKJV)?

10. Is worry a sin?

II. Of all the various topics Paul mentions here (resolving conflicts with others, rejoicing, showing gentleness, remembering the imminent return of the Lord, praying about situations), which would bring more peace to your life?

LIFE LESSONS

Can you think of anything the world needs more than peace? Look around your neighborhood at all the squabbling spouses and fractured friendships. Listen to people at work talk about their restless, stressful lives. Watch the news and see the tragic victims of crime and war, hear the litany of scary reports of disease and doom. As Christians we have the opportunity (and the responsibility) to show the world a different and better way. How? By living in peace with our fellow Christians. By trusting God to pour out his incomprehensible peace in life's anxious times. And by never forgetting the words of Jesus, "Those who work to bring peace are happy, because God will call them his children." (Matt. 5:9 NCV).

DEVOTION

Lord, fill me with a desire for unity. Fill me with joy. Fill me with gentleness and kindness and the firm conviction that your return is soon. Fill me with a thankful spirit and a consuming desire to seek you. And when I am filled with all these things, there will be no room in my heart for worry.

For more Bible passages on experiencing God's peace, see Proverbs 15:1; Isaiah 26:3; Luke 12:25–26; Romans 12:16–18; Colossians 2:2; 1 Thessalonians 5:13; and 1 Peter 5:7.

To complete the book of Philippians during this twelve-part study, read Philippians 4:1–7.

JOURNALING

List all the things (relationships, situations, trials, etc.) that stress you out, and by each one list what you can realistically do about it.

IT'S ALL IN YOUR MIND

MAX
LUCADO

REFLECTION

Change. Don't we all need a makeover? Worrywarts need peace; those who struggle with greed or envy need to learn the art of contentment. Truth be told, most folks *hunger* to be different in various big and small ways. So, here is one of the most valuable questions we could ever ponder . . . how *do* people change?

SITUATION

Writing from a Roman prison to his beloved Christian friends in Philippi who are struggling to live for Christ and to grow in their faith, Paul shares the truth that a healthy, God-honoring lifestyle begins with a healthy, God-honoring mind-set.

OBSERVATION

Read Philippians 4:8–13 from the NCV or the NKJV.

NCV

8Brothers and sisters, think about the things that are good and worthy of praise. Think about the things that are true and honorable and right and pure and beautiful and respected. 9Do what you learned and received from me, what I told you, and what you saw me do. And the God who gives peace will be with you.

10I am very happy in the Lord that you have shown your care for me again. You continued to care about me, but there was no way for you to show it. 11I am not telling you this because I need anything. I have learned to be satisfied with the things I have and with everything that happens. 12I know how to live when I am poor, and I know how to live when I have plenty. I have learned the secret of being happy at any time in everything that happens, when I have enough to eat and when I go hungry, when I have more than I need and when I do not have enough. 13I can do all things through Christ, because he gives me strength.

NKJV

8Finally, brethren, whatever things are true, whatever things are noble, whatever things are just, whatever things are pure, whatever things are lovely, whatever things are of good report, if there is any virtue and if there is anything praiseworthy—meditate on these things. 9The things which you learned and received and heard and saw in me, these do, and the God of peace will be with you.

10But I rejoiced in the Lord greatly that now at last your care for me has flourished again; though you surely did care, but you lacked opportunity. 11Not that I speak in regard to need, for I have learned in whatever state I am, to be content: 12I know how to be abased, and I know how to abound. Everywhere and in all things I have learned both to be full and to be hungry, both to abound and to suffer need. 13I can do all things through Christ who strengthens me.

EXPLORATION

1. Why are our thoughts so important?

2. What is significant about the qualities Paul chose for evaluating and ordering one's thoughts?

3. What conclusions, if any, should we draw from the fact that Paul speaks about thinking in verse 8 and about doing in verse 9?

4. Paul seems to be suggesting that when our thinking is spiritually sound, our circumstances will stop stealing our joy. How can this be? Have you experienced this in your life?

5. What true thought strengthened Paul and enabled him to be content during hard circumstances and times of want?

INSPIRATION

You and I are infected by destructive thoughts. Computer viruses have names like Klez, Anna Kournikova, and ILOVEYOU. Mental viruses are known as anxiety, bitterness, anger, guilt, shame, greed, and insecurity. They worm their way into your system and diminish, even disable, your mind. We call these DTPs: destructive thought patterns. (Actually, I'm the only one to call them DTPs.)

Do you have any DTPs?

When you see the successful, are you jealous?

When you see the struggler, are you pompous?

If someone gets on your bad side, is that person as likely to get on your good side as I am to win the Tour-de-France?

Ever argue with someone in your mind? Rehash or rehearse your hurts? Do you assume the worst about the future?

If so, you suffer from DTPs.

What would your world be like without them? Had no dark or destructive thought ever entered your mind, how would you be different? Suppose you could live your life sans any guilt, lust, vengeance, insecurity, or fear. Never wasting mental energy on gossip or scheming. Would you be different? . . .

Oh, to be DTP-free. No energy lost, no time wasted. Wouldn't such a person be energetic and wise? A lifetime of healthy and holy thoughts would render any-one a joyful genius . . .

A lot like the twelve-year-old boy seated in the temple of Jerusalem. Though he was beardless and unadorned, this boy's thoughts were profound . . . When it comes to his purity of mind, we are given this astounding claim: Christ "knew no sin" (2 Cor. 5:21 NKJV). Peter says Jesus "did no sin, neither was guile found in his mouth" (1 Pet. 2:22 KJV). John lived next to him for three years and con-cluded, "In Him there is no sin" (1 John 3:5 NKJV) . . .

But does this matter? Does the perfection of Christ affect me? If he were a distant Creator, the answer would be no. But since he is a next door Savior, the reply is a supersized yes!

Remember the twelve-year-old boy in the temple? The one with sterling thoughts and a Teflon mind? Guess what. That is God's goal for you! You are made to be like Christ! God's priority is that you be "transformed by the renew-ing of your mind" (Rom. 12:2 NIV). You may have been born virus-prone, but you don't have to live that way . . . God can change your mind. (From *Next Door Savior* by Max Lucado)

REACTION

6. What are some of your destructive thought patterns?

7. It seems as though Paul is advocating a kind of Christian form of meditation. What do you think of this?

8. How disciplined is your mind—that is, do you work at corralling untrue and unhealthy thoughts?

9. How confident would you be telling a younger Christian what Paul told the Philippians in verse 9? Why?

10. Are you a contented person?

11. How much are your moods dependent on your circumstances?

LIFE LESSONS

Mention *meditation* and most Christians either glaze over or tense up. Perhaps you, too, view this practice as incomprehensible or even incompatible with your faith. But in fact meditation is both described and prescribed in Scripture (Josh. 1:8; Ps. 119:27). At the most basic level, meditation is simply focusing one's mind on a thought or set of thoughts. It is chewing on an idea like a cow might chew its cud. It is letting our minds marinate in (i.e., soak up) a certain idea. We all do this. Even worrying is a (negative) form of meditating—it is dwelling on possible bad outcomes. Paul is telling us here that the path to a joy-filled life of contentment and peace is by learning to meditate on what God says is true. Will you do this today?

DEVOTION

Father, I have so much to learn. I realize that my mind is often focused on things that are untrue, unworthy, unlovely, and unhealthy. By your Spirit, teach me how to reprogram my thoughts so that they line up with yours. Impress upon me the great truth that my life will never change until my mind is changed.

For more Bible passages on renewing your mind, see Psalm 119:15, 48, 78, 97, 99; 143:5; Romans 12:1–2; and 2 Corinthians 10:3–6.

To complete the book of Philippians during this twelve-part study, read Philippians 4:8–13.

JOURNALING

Think back over the last forty-eight hours and zero in on an incident in which you got extremely emotional (panicky, angry, depressed, etc.). What thoughts contributed to your strong feelings? How do those thoughts compare with what God says is true?

LESSON TWELVE

GENEROSITY

MAX
LUCADO

REFLECTION

Gifts. At birthdays, weddings, anniversaries, births, graduations, and holidays, we give and receive presents. It's hard to imagine a world without this practice. Are you more comfortable giving or receiving gifts? Why?

SITUATION

Philippians is an inspired thank-you note from the apostle Paul to the Macedonian believers who had supported him with several generous financial gifts. Paul uses this correspondence to remind the Philippians of many important biblical truths, and then he concludes with a sincere expression of appreciation and some thoughts on giving.

OBSERVATION

Read Philippians 4:14–23 from the NCV or the NKJV.

NCV

[14]But it was good that you helped me when I needed it. [15]You Philippians remember when I first preached the Good News there. When I left Macedonia, you were the only church that gave me help. [16]Several times you sent me things I needed when I was in Thessalonica. [17]Really, it is not that I want to receive gifts from you, but I want you to have the good that comes from giving. [18]And now I have everything, and more. I have all I need, because Epaphroditus brought your gift to me. It is like a sweet-smelling sacrifice offered to God, who accepts that sacrifice and is pleased with it. [19]My God will use his wonderful riches in Christ Jesus to give you everything you need. [20]Glory to our God and Father forever and ever! Amen.

[21]Greet each of God's people in Christ. Those who are with me send greetings to you. [22]All of God's people greet you, particularly those from the palace of Caesar.

[23]The grace of the Lord Jesus Christ be with you all.

NKJV

¹⁴*Nevertheless you have done well that you shared in my distress.* ¹⁵*Now you Philippians know also that in the beginning of the gospel, when I departed from Macedonia, no church shared with me concerning giving and receiving but you only.* ¹⁶*For even in Thessalonica you sent aid once and again for my necessities.* ¹⁷*Not that I seek the gift, but I seek the fruit that abounds to your account.* ¹⁸*Indeed I have all and abound. I am full, having received from Epaphroditus the things sent from you, a sweet-smelling aroma, an acceptable sacrifice, well pleasing to God.* ¹⁹*And my God shall supply all your need according to His riches in glory by Christ Jesus.* ²⁰*Now to our God and Father be glory forever and ever. Amen.*

²¹*Greet every saint in Christ Jesus. The brethren who are with me greet you.* ²²*All the saints greet you, but especially those who are of Caesar's household.*

²³*The grace of our Lord Jesus Christ be with you all. Amen.*

EXPLORATION

1. What were the Philippians' giving habits?

2. Though Paul's comment in verse 17 may sound trite, what does he mean by it?

3. Paul writes of "the good that comes from giving" (v. 17 NCV). What good comes to the giver?

4. What determines whether a gift gets praised (as in this case) or is scorned by God (see Proverbs 15:8; Isaiah 1:10–17; and Malachi 1:8)?

5. What is the promise to those who give with the right attitude?

INSPIRATION

Today I will make a difference. I will begin by controlling my thoughts. A person is the product of his thoughts. I want to be happy and hopeful. Therefore, I will have thoughts that are happy and hopeful. I refuse to be victimized by my circumstances. I will not let petty inconveniences such as stoplights, long lines, and traffic jams be my masters. I will avoid negativism and gossip. Optimism will be my companion, and victory will be my hallmark. Today I will make a difference.

I will be grateful for the twenty-four hours that are before me. Time is a precious commodity. I refuse to allow what little time I have to be contaminated by self-pity, anxiety, or boredom. I will face this day with the joy of a child and the courage of a giant. I will drink each minute as though it is my last. When tomorrow comes, today will be gone forever. While it is here, I will use it for loving and giving. Today I will make a difference.

I will not let past failures haunt me. Even though my life is scarred with mistakes, I refuse to rummage through my trash heap of failures. I will admit them. I will correct them. I will press on. Victoriously. No failure is fatal. It's OK to stumble; I will get up. It's OK to fail; I will rise again. Today I will make a difference.

I will spend time with those I love. My spouse, my children, my family. A man can own the world but be poor for the lack of love. A man can own nothing and yet be wealthy in relationships. Today I will spend at least five minutes with the significant people in my world. Five *quality* minutes of talking or hugging or thanking or listening. Five undiluted minutes with my mate, children, and friends.

Today I will make a difference. (From *On the Anvil* by Max Lucado)

REACTION

6. Can our small gifts and offerings really make a difference?

7. In supporting Paul, the Philippians were literally supporting a missionary. What are the implications of this for you and your church?

8. Many people feel that churches overly emphasize giving. Is this a fair assessment?

9. If God doesn't really need our money (see Psalm 50), why does the Bible say so much about giving?

10. What are your giving habits—do you give regularly and generously?

11. Is tithing an Old Testament practice only, or are all Christians required to give 10 percent?

LIFE LESSONS

The Bible is clear. Money is a blessing, a danger, a stewardship, a test, and a tool. And what we do with material wealth is a reliable indicator of our spiritual health. How we behave with money reveals what we truly believe. If we are tight-fisted, if we hoard, if we think constantly of getting and spending but only rarely of giving, we disclose that we do not really trust God's goodness, that we do not have faith that God's supplies are infinite. At issue in this area of giving is not the amount but our attitude. Do we see giving as a duty or a delight? Do we give grudgingly or with joy? Hear again the challenge of Jesus—to use your worldly wealth for his eternal purposes (Luke 16:1–13).

DEVOTION

Lord, teach me the paradoxical truth that the way I "get a grip" on this subject of giving is by "loosening my grip" on my money. Amaze me over and over with how generous you have been with me, so that I might willingly and gladly pass on your blessings to others.

For more Bible passages on generosity, see Deuteronomy 16:17; 1 Chronicles 29:9; Proverbs 3:9; Matthew 10:8; Acts 11:29; and 2 Corinthians 8:12; 9:7.

To complete the book of Philippians during this twelve-part study, read Philippians 4:14–23.

JOURNALING

Imagine a face-to-face conversation with Jesus, with your financial records spread out between you. What do you imagine he might say to you about the way you use the resources he has entrusted you with?

Lucado Life
Lesson Series

*Revised and updated, the Lucado Life Lessons series is perfect
for small group or individual use and includes intriguing questions
that will take you deeper into God's Word.*

Available at your local Christian Bookstore.